## PRAISE FOR *SCAR AND FLOWER*

"This is an incredible, luminous and most serious investigation, of being, of human suffering, of war and peace—of the factories of violence and the notebook of enlightenments. We deepen into spirit and lives lost. Lee is concerned with the turning of beauty, the intimacy of death and the boundlessness of small moments, 'the broken body of a tiny bird,' fragments that can change a life. Glitterings of light, planetary systems, electric skies available and unavailable. He is the 'form rider' of hope. A stellar project, here. Rare and gifted, a timely arrival. Life-deep brilliance."

—Juan Felipe Herrera,
U.S. Poet Laureate (2015-2017)

"Lee Herrick is a poet of the ecstatic. In this collection, he reminds us that the body has its own light-filled astronomy, that the body is also a torrent of terror and desire. Here are furious elegies about the way America is on fire with its bombs and guns and false prayers. Herrick gathers stray echoes, a myriad of birds, the motherless ocean, and much more into much more into a dreamy symphony dedicated to the deep hum of our collective grief. And yet, so much love. This poet is an unapologetic patriot in the vast country of love, a place of abundance in the aching language of both scars and flowers."

—Sun Yung Shin

"Lee Herrick's visionary, ocean-hearted third collection stares down the forces sweeping through North America—and dares to listen to the howl. Here is the father dreaming despite daily violence in a country under siege. *Scar and Flower* crosses continents and oceans, translates moonlight, and reckons with what it means to be alive, and lost, and in love with fire-light at the beginning of the 21st century. From bullets to bonfires, daughter-love and a farmer's *ars poetica*, the landscapes conjured here haunt our waking dreams, much like the boy with a gun who wanders, painfully, through these pages. All the while, Herrick's singular voice and vision propels us forward—sound over sound, rose over rose—as if to say: motion is resistance, and listening, the one true act of grace. A mighty, tender, and fearless book from a poet at the height of his powers."

—Brynn Saito

# PRAISE FOR *GARDENING SECRETS OF THE DEAD*

"These gorgeously rendered snapshots—a disarming fusion of lyric and meticulous narrative—are clearly the work of a true storyteller, a master of focus and fearlessness. There is a whole life lurking within these stanzas, a life that Herrick masterfully unreels in his role as witness, during which he manages to be both the 'other' and all of us. If there was even a modicum of doubt about this poet's enviable talent, or his place among those who've crafted a singular creative signature, *Gardening Secrets of the Dead* will lay that indecision to rest."

—Patricia Smith

"Lee Herrick's *Gardening Secrets of the Dead* is a lyric exploration of the fractured and fragmented landscape of the self, where the body is a song composed of many selves. Whitman revised, the poems 'celebrate and assemble / from around the world' with a voice that is politically engaged and rooted in compassion. *Gardening Secrets of the Dead* is a wise, gorgeous book—one steeped in the deeply human process of living in what is often an untenable world, where we are instructed to 'breathe as if your chest is an ocean.' A poet's poet, Herrick's work is a gift for us all."

—Brian Turner

"In this illuminated collection of poems, Lee Herrick's tempered, yet fearless, voice presents us with a contemplative space—fertile earth—in which to gather the tiny crystals of our life and piece them back into the light inherent in us all. Because there is light here, in each well-crafted line, in the departures and returns, the remembering and the letting go, every last letter a tender 'gift of rage and lilacs.' Here is a poet in love with the world—its failures, fires and faith—and *Gardening Secrets of the Dead* is his testimony."

—Tim Z. Hernandez

# Praise for *This Many Miles from Desire*

"The universal sadness, almost Sufi-like, and the timeless compassion these poems articulate make it possible for a reader to believe that any 'I' must include the whole world, inside and out, bliss and pain, broken and whole. I love these poems."

—Li-Young Lee

"Lee's poems bend towards light, towards a higher grace beyond words. Here is a collection of wise, heartfelt, honest poems that feel like songs, sad songs you play alone at midnight to remind your soul to live. Yes. Live. It will be one of my new travel bibles to take on the road, to comfort me when I get weary, to remind me that what we are doing is priceless and soulful and necessary as prayer. Bless you, Lee, for this beautiful music."

—Ishle Yi Park

"Lee Herrick's poems celebrate the ability to make a life in the awkward space between worlds, where we find ourselves 'not quite the rose / but not quite the roots.' In settings as diverse as Korea, Latin America, and Fresno, California, the poems speak of the emotional experience of being adopted, of one man's search for identity, of the problem of abandonment—but most of all, they speak of the constancy of love. There is no blame or bitterness here at all. These are songs of grace and acceptance and joy, and they invite us to open our arms and embrace the complexities of our own unstable worlds. This is a poet with enormous talent and a large and generous heart."

—Corrinne Clegg Hales

"Lee Herrick's debut collection, *This Many Miles from Desire*, makes you stop and think about everything you've assumed before. As a Korean adoptee, Herrick stretches, deepens, and illuminates our previous notions of mother (both maternal and national identity), father, God, lover. The poems which emanate from the poet's Fresno home to journeys to Seoul, China, Southeast Asia, Latin America, radiate a lovely sensuality grounded in an earthy, humbling wisdom. In the book's closing lines, Herrick talks about the sacred— as in 'the moment when she touched / your bare arm for the first time, her fingers / like cool flashes of heaven.'"

—Amy Uyematsu

Published by Gunpowder Press
David Starkey, Editor
PO Box 60035
Santa Barbara, CA 93160-0035

Cover image: Lisa Lee Herrick

ISBN-13: 978-1-957062-17-4

Library of Congress Control Number: 2024914166

www.gunpowderpress.com

Gunpowder Press books are published by Gunpowder Poetry, a 501(c)(3) nonprofit literary organization based in Santa Barbara, California.

# In Praise of Late Wonder

## New and Selected Poems

## Lee Herrick

Gunpowder Press • Santa Barbara
2024

*For Lisa*

*For Suzhen*

*For adoptees everywhere*

# CONTENTS

STARS

### From *Scar and Flower* (2019)

STARS

## Whiteness

When I was nine years old, in Modesto, California, I took a shower before bed. I locked the bathroom door and began to shampoo my hair. I looked down at my brown skin, wet and glistening. I wondered why I was not white. I rolled the bar of soap into a light blue washcloth until it was lathered in suds, and I began to rub it into my forearm. Softly at first. Then, harder. I wondered if I could turn my skin white. Of course, I couldn't. My skin was brown. I stopped after a couple of minutes, rinsed myself entirely, and wrapped myself in a towel.

I scrubbed my skin because I wondered why I was not white. This is different than wanting to *be* white. I have never wanted to be white. But because I was raised in a white family, and this was the era of "color-blindness" translated as open-minded and accepting rather than damaging and dismissive, I wondered why I looked one way and my family, whom I loved, looked entirely different. I wondered why I was not white as much as I wondered why they weren't Korean. It was confusing, but we were family—a collection of people who love but don't always understand who we are or how we came to be.

## Sadness

My sadness began on the day I was born. I don't say this to be melodramatic, but it's true. Or what might be more true is that I inherited my first mother's and father's sadnesses, which must be serious since neither has met me, or they died before they met me, or maybe my first father doesn't know I exist. They must be regularly sad, vacant, or dreaming. What do you call a sadness you embody but do not know you embody? Sadness felt like something else when I was living it—anxiety, fear, even paralysis. These were the manifestations, but sadness and loss were the foundation. It can also look like something different—good grades, world travel. If I were to describe it in its purest form, though, mine was like staring into a dark blue, almost black night, full of muted stars I couldn't name. Somehow, though, and it probably has a lot to do with poetry and music, I came out the other side with a joy that no person or thing can ever take away.

# Home

I was born sometime in late 1970 in South Korea. Daejeon, I believe. When I was under five months old, I may have been homeless. I never thought of it this way until recently, but if the stories of my adoption are true, I may have been homeless for a very short time, maybe just an hour or a few minutes, at a police station, church, or the Daejeon Christian Social Center, where I was reportedly found. I sat on the cold steps or the cold street, perhaps in basket with a sky-blue blanket. Or, maybe I was never without a home. Maybe none of us is ever without a home if we re-envision it—not as an address, a zip code, or a welcome mat at the front door—but being loved and being able to be ourselves, *at home*, if you will. Or, if planet earth is home, we are at home until we leave for the next realm, which is merely another home. Somewhere in late 1970, there was a home in great distress: the home of my birth mother's body, my birth father's clouded heart, and the room in Korea where I was born, with a head full of hair, a side-eye already developed, and a fire in my heart that would burn for a lifetime.

## Mother Clouds

If my dead birth parents are clouds, floating over their countries and drifting into others, I am a cloud, too. In the shape of a moon. Tree. Half-moon, mangled heart. The World Meteorological Association tells us that clouds often form or grow from other clouds, called mother clouds. There are two kinds of mother clouds: genitus, where a part of a cloud may develop, and more or less pronounced extensions may form; and mutatus, where the whole or a large part of a cloud may undergo complete internal transformation, changing from one genus into another. So, my body, my being, my seemingly birth parent-less self is a cloud, too. This is why I float. Even mountains and rocks change form and mutate. But I've always felt most at home near the water and looking up into the sky, where most any day I'll see at least a few clouds. A cloud is a hydrometeor, made of minute particles of water and ice, sometimes with particles of fumes, smoke or dust. I imagine my birth parents had some particles of fumes, smoke or dust. I am fumes, smoke, or dust then, too.

# Idea

A friend told me once that being adopted feels like you were never born at all. I sat in my recliner at home in Fresno and thought about what she said. It makes sense because I don't know the day I was born, nor the exact place—city, hospital, living room, or field. If I was never born, it might explain why I sometimes feel more like an idea than a person. What I mean to say is that it took me a long time to feel what some scholars have called being human: to feel, to lose, to dream.

# Wonder

For a period of time in my late twenties, I once thought every Korean woman 15 to 50 years older than me could be my mother. I'd imagine walking up to her and asking, *Did you ever give birth to a boy and then lose him or give him away*? The classy businesswoman wearing expensive shoes, the dry cleaner who wanted to teach me Korean, the woman who shoved kimchi in my mouth and said hers was the best in Seoul. The homeless one. I could be part of each one. This lasted for about five years until I realized I was wrong, that not knowing who a woman was did not mean she was likely who I thought. I began to study logic and reason and devoured philosophy. I began to see Korean women as a source of pride and strength and wholeness rather than a mystery or a curse. I began to see people everywhere around the planet in full dimension rather than through my singular and limited lens. This changed everything.

# Writing

I only have a few documents from my adoption. Most are typed on thin rice paper, folded over several times. My parents kept them in a blue baby book titled "All About You," stuffed with grade school ribbons, class photographs of the twenty-nine white kids and me, the first poem I wrote in third grade titled "Football," and pictures from camping trips or birthdays. One of them is my intake report, which describes my personality as a five-month old. When you don't have a parent or anyone who knew you in your life at that time, paper, stories, another person's written recollection is priceless. Their impression, their version, their decisions shaped my identity and how I saw and how I see myself to this day. I have so much faith in writing. Not because it's necessarily truth but because it's true that someone wrote it, thought it, believed it, and therefore archived an important truth. A signature, a date, a description. Lee Kwang Soo: shy around strangers. Likes to smile.

## Stars

I am one of approximately 200,000 Korean adoptees or adopted Koreans in the entire world. A small subset of the 83 million Koreans. Other small populations like ours include the Ambonese from Indonesia, Blaan of Philippines, Damara from Namibia, Sioux, Lakota from the US, and Otomi from Mexico. We're rare. Like shooting stars. Double rainbows. Scratched diamonds.

# Daejeon

One day, a videographer and translator and I went to Daejeon to make a short film. I was an American author, so a television station thought it make a good story and give my search some exposure. Perhaps alert a family member who would remember me that I was here, that I was alive, that I had not vanished into the ether of another country's clouds. The videographer was thin but athletic, like a swimmer, with fluffy hair that looked like he'd spent three days straight in a dark editing room pulling at his hair. He was kind but very focused on his work. I'd come to wonder later if he was also quiet because he had misgivings about the day's work. Maybe he felt it wasn't generous or purely noble but rather, it might be tinged with a hint of what all modern media becomes: exploitative. There's a condition where the human spirit reaches a point of exasperation, or desperation, or confusion, that establishes the conditions for exploitation, which also requires a dose of naiveté or being unaware. I was always a small bit of both, but here in Daejeon, overwhelmed with decades of loss, anger, and confusion about my birth family, I didn't realize the exploitative elements of what we were doing. I only thought it was a good idea, and I thought there was a chance, albeit a very small one, that it would lead to meeting my birth family. This was before DNA testing, before I overcame desperation.

We went to a shopping mall. It wasn't a modern mall with high end or even chain shops, but it overflowed with teens in school uniforms, Korean-style chain gadgets dangling from their phones, so much laughter and snacking. We shot for about two hours. The one I remember most is the long, slow, solemn stroll—how he told me to look up and off into the distance as if I were looking at the stars. As I walked through the crowded mall, the teenage girls wondering who I was, I did as he instructed. As he filmed, I walked, forlorn and trying to act composed, but all I wanted to do was break down and cry. Breathe for a short while, then cry again.

# Holt

In April 2008, I walked alone to the Holt Offices in Seoul, Korea. It was a few days before I went on "I Miss You" on KBS. There was a young, White, hetero couple walking in front of me. They were excited about their new son. They were in their late 20's probably, which made them ten years younger than me as I walked into the building where social workers must know someone like me means, what—trouble? Threat? A long day? I was there to get my adoption paperwork. I was weak from thirty years of loss and sadness. I entered the building, as the young couple left. I got lost in the building. I floated in my anxiety. The children's posters on the wall unnerved me. A Korean woman in her thirties, sleek mid-length straight hair, and a red skirt and a white blouse smiled at me and welcomed me. She led me into a small room that was bare except for a square table with two chairs on opposite sides. In the middle of the table sat a box of tissues. I thought, I don't need those. They knew, though. Of course I would need them.

She asked me a few questions in English. Name. Date of birth. Why I was there. Who I'd spoken to in the United States or in Seoul. It almost felt like an interrogation. All that was missing was the heat lamp and the two-way mirror. In retrospect, there may have been a two-way mirror.

I wanted to tell her, you know why I'm here. I could barely breathe, though. She left me in the small room as she went to get my file. I sat there, broken and simple. I wondered, *would they have my real name? Would they know where I was born and found? Would they know my parents' names?*

When she came back into the room, I must have looked as white as the paper she held. She showed me only the first page of what seemed to be about seven to ten pages. On the bottom of the first page, she drew my attention to a few boxes that had been covered with white tape, and I assumed these were my parents' real names. I couldn't believe the social worker concealed them, but she said I couldn't see it. She seemed cold but resigned. I began to cry. It was an involuntary and deep welling up of liquified God, a reckoning. There was not much she could do at that point. This was 2008, years before changes to the laws, to the commonplace DNA testing, to the rights of adopted people to see their own information. I sat weeping softly for a minute or two, wiped my nose and my eyes, stood up and softly left the building. The light outside was bright, and the young couple were gone, off to start a new life. I was, too. I'd made a pilgrimage and become a new light. It would be several years before I realized it, but I became a new person that day—no longer helpless, no longer passive. I had gone to Korea to ask for my file. I had gone to Korea to ask for my life. It would impact my life back in the United States, my troubled marriage, and my basic sense of self. I had a right to live and discovered I had a right to be loved.

# Searching

The Korean television show hosts were gorgeous, their skin like satin clouds and affluence. I was in Seoul to search for birth family. KBS, South Korea's largest and most popular television station, aired a morning television program called "I Miss You," a show about lost family members and reunions. My friend, the writer Kim Sunée, was being filmed for a documentary about her adoption from Korea and told me that the director, her friend Roy, could get me on the show. This was 2008, and I had gone 38 years of my life not thinking of searching for birth family, and within a week, I had decided to go for it, thrust into a major television studio. During the pre-show taping, the translator offered me a balm he said would soothe my nerves, but I felt like I was going to pass out, so I declined, fighting the lightheadedness. I sat in the back row of two rows of Koreans looking for family. I didn't speak the language. I was 38 and hoping someone would recognize me, my story, or come claim me. In all, there were eight of us, looking into the bright lights in the tv studio.

The transnational birth family search can often be an insurmountable wall of dead-ends, emotional re-traumatization, and despair. The jarring shift into full-speed ahead birth family search in such a public way left me somewhat used by the program for ratings. Before the taping, KBS tests your DNA, in case a family member comes forward and thinks you are family. The gorgeous young hosts asked me *What would you like to say to your birth mother? Why are you searching for your family?* Somehow, I didn't faint during the show, but I can't remember much of it. After the show ended, I waited for weeks to hear if anyone called in to the show. I imagined an aunt saying she recognized my baby photo. I imagined a man, full of shame or light, saying *I am your father*. I imagined my birth mother running toward me, speaking in a language I don't understand but in a way that I knew to mean, *I am your mother. I have never stopped loving you.*

But none of this happened I waited months, then a year, then I realized it would probably never happen. I did not find my birth family. I did not have a tearful reunion with my Korean mother and father. But I was able to put to rest the questions and holes I thought once might kill me. I found light where there was none before. I came out the other side. I realized that we adoptees are always whole, despite missing parts of our origin stories. I was whole then; I'm whole now, whatever our searches reveal or uncover.

# Photograph

Adopted Koreans come from a range of experiences—wrong names and wrong identities, kidnapping, and mostly, unwed mothers. I only have one picture of myself before the age of 1 year old. I have a full head of hair. I look as if I know it is going to be a long life full of difficulty and joy. There's a number on a placard on my chest—#9143. There's a loud Korean heartbeat in my chest.

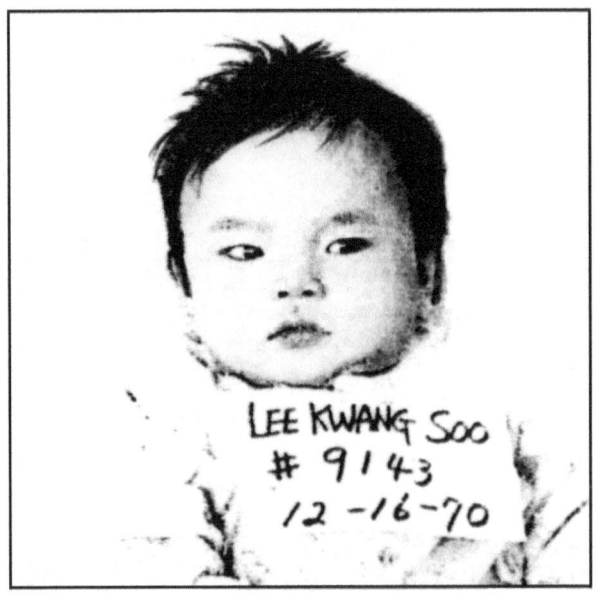

Lee (Korean name Lee Kwang Soo) in South Korea, 1971, just before he was adopted to the United States. Courtesy of the Author.

## Idea #2

I am not the fairly-tale, the golden ticket story of the adoption reunion, the boy/man reunited with his birth/first mother after two, three, or four decades. Rather, I am one who should've gone adrift but didn't, the one who survived, the one who despite having no answers, no certain birthdate, birthplace, birth father, or birth mother, the one who found joy. I used to wonder how was I even born. But I'm here. I survived. I am the idea that did not detonate.

# Phillip Clay

Phillip Clay was adopted to the United States from Korea when he was eight years old. He grew up in Philadelphia. He committed a drug-related misdemeanor as an adult close to my age, and by virtue of a terrible loophole in our immigration laws, he was deported back to South Korea, where he knew no one, had no family, and could not speak the language. Soon thereafter, Phillip committed suicide. He jumped from the 14th story of a building in Seoul—suicide, a hundred flowers burst into hundreds more, the blinding sun. Approximately 34,000 people commit suicide each year, roughly one every fifteen minutes. Adoptees are four time more likely to evaporate like this. I try to imagine how shattered and irreparable Phillip must have felt, or perhaps he was numb, blank. I don't know. I'll never know.

The year after his suicide, at an adoption conference in San Francisco where I was the keynote speaker, I met John, who brought Phillip's ashes back to Philadelphia, where he grew up after being adopted, where his adoptive parents refused to attend his memorial. I was asked to write a poem for Phillip's service, which I did. I have seen pictures of Phillip, and you can't see the internal rattling in his soul. But I know that sound. Mine was a slightly lower volume. When I was eighteen or nineteen, I thought about suicide, but the thought alone scared me out of it. I thought like this for a month or so, imagined the method (running car in the garage, jumping) and reaction, which I thought would range from sadness and surprise to nothing, as I thought some people I'd hoped would care wouldn't even notice. But I knew in my gut that it would hurt my mother and father, and I couldn't manage that idea. The deep well of despair, of being lost with no belief or faith in someday being found, suicide is not a myth. It is embedded fabric, a blotted note. It is Phillip Clay's earthward body through the afternoon sky in Seoul.

# Home

Home is the space around your heart, like a moat, so that the space in your heart, or your spirit, can have room to breathe. To be and become more of who you are. We know at a young age what hurts—rocks, name calling, being ignored. Over time, some remain and some change, as home might. But we must protect our home, our identities, what we know to be most true. Within that there's a lot of space, in my home at least, for discovery, risk, exploration, and safe argument. One could say that's a class or economic luxury, and they'd be right. But I'd say space is always important—space in your heart, room in your mind.

When I say I might have missed my birth mother and father every day of my life, I mean that as a person of color raised in a white family, I was constantly and acutely aware of physical difference and what that could mean. Along with home and country and family and language, as a child I was separated from the right to grieve. Adoption as a one-dimensional, one-way avenue toward gratitude and fortune is illogical and harmful. I recently read a book by a noted novelist whose father died when she was in her fifties. She was, understandably, grieving. She said, how do I continue with such an absence? I thought, here is the adopted person's situation from infancy. This loss, this massive absence, is thrust upon them from the moment of separation. I call it an inverted grief thrust upon the adoptee.

Home is where you are understood or loved or able to be weird. Strange. Confused. Your lost self. Your full, human, self. Mostly, I felt at home. Sometimes, I felt like so alone I could almost vanish.

# Names

## Names I Have Been Made to Feel

1.  Chink
2.  Ching-chong
3.  Gook
4.  Chinaman
5.  Chop Suey
6.  Bruce Lee
7.  Slant Eye
8.  Squinty Eye
9.  Chino
10. Jap
11. Kung-flu

# Questions

Questions I've Been Asked by Total Strangers (Intrusion Masked as Curiosity)

1.    Have you been back to Korea?
2.    Have you met your birth parents?
3.    Do you know why they gave you up?
4.    Are you from the North or the South?
5.    Do you speak Korean?
6.    Do you like kimchi?
7.    Have you found your birth family?
8.    Who would you want to win in a war, Korea or the U.S.?
9.    Don't you feel lucky?

# Adoption

Adoption is a wildfire, glass lake, steep mountain.

Adopt, adapt, adaptation, adoption, adopted, adoptee, adulation, adoration, adult, adept, adopter, adoptive, adopt-a-pet, adopt a textbook, readopt, Hollywood adoption distortion Iron Man, Spider-Man, Superman, Annie, The Jerk, Punky Brewster, and Margo, Edith, and Agnes from Despicable Me, meme, memory, magically, mystery, we who miss, we who magic, we who breathe so deep like this.

To *re-member* is to become wholly functional action, to join the group again, to re-body, to mem-oir, to re-create, to re-verse, to re-collect, to re-mind, to re-sist, to re-habilitate, re-cover, re-establish, re-form. To write is to form again, establish again, to exist again. Adoption is to mind again, verse again, to build, store, create, and live again.

# Idea #3

A Korean adoptee friend showed me her slightly scarred and deformed ear. She said a rat or some other animal had been eating her when she was found in a trash bin. She now works with the transgender community in her hometown. One Korean adoptee wrote about being taken to a busy outdoor market at age eight by his mother and aunt, who told him to start walking and not to turn around and look at them, just keep walking. He did as he was told. Eventually he turned around to look for them, and in a cloud of faces and bustling shoppers, they were gone. He was instantly homeless, a street kid at eight years old. By nightfall, other street kids had beaten him up and taken his new shoes. By morning, he was a fighter, a miracle, the beginning of his own future idea. He now holds over 50 U.S. medical patents and founded a medical services company. Once, he donated over one million dollars to Korean adoptees who could not afford DNA kits to research their family histories. Once, each of us was in Korea. In a new country, each of us became beautiful and did something beautiful, even if only once.

# Gratitude

Adoptees are often asked to appreciate and silence our own trauma. I am not grateful that I lost my Korean family. I am not grateful that I do not know the woman who gave birth to me or the man who fathered me. When you ask if I am grateful to have been adopted, I will tell you about a hundred shapes of clouds in most any sky. I am grateful that the two people who adopted me were Newby and Georgia Herrick. This is different than being grateful to be adopted. If God's will is what will be, and later I will tell you how I found God to always be with me and therefore I believe deeply in God, then my adoption was written in the stars long before I became human. It was part of my first mother's inevitable questions. It could trace back to my Korean mother's tuberculosis, her unwed life, her own mother's suicide or other stories that I fabricate like a magician.

# Soju

To discover the traditional and popular alcohol of your birth country is like entering an ancient painting and touching a fraction of the great artists' madness. Soju, maekkoli, oils, brushes. What enters us stays with us, even if only in dreams. Eventually I learned some of the language of my country's food and drink — the jujube tea, the silk worms, the barbecue, the grilled squid sold on the street in the small white bags. Of course, the kimchi. How it heals and soothes, comforts and inspires. When I was in Seoul in 2008, my friend the writer Jane Jeong Trenka had organized a reading for me at KoRoot, the guesthouse for Korean adoptees from around the world. You can imagine the rush and the nerves reading in your home country 37 years after you left. Pastor Kim, the esteemed gentleman who runs the guesthouse with his wife, introduced me. The audience was small, maybe 15 people, but one of them was a woman I'd met in China a few years prior, a large woman in her sixties. She was in Seoul after having met a man during her travels, and she'd come to live there for a few months. There was a Korean professor who'd published a scholarly article on my poetry. And then there was Leah. She was in her twenties, and she was from the East Coast in the United States. She was a college undergrad with a sharp curiosity and hunger in her eye, and we connected over poetry and adoptee life. Years later, when she was completing her MFA in Poetry at the University of Miami, she asked me to be on her MFA thesis committee, which the chair approved. In 2015, we discovered through DNA testing that we are *related*. By blood. If you aren't an adoptee, the phrase "by blood" might not mean much if it's your norm, but for us, for me, for those bright stars like us, it's a lifelong source of longing and desire. Knowing Leah in this life, this kind of connection, calms me every time I think about it. Meeting biological relatives makes me float through the world a little lower, slightly more grounded.

# Dear Korean Mother,

~~Some time approximately~~ Around 50 years ago, I was born, and ~~I believe~~ you are my mother. Eomeoni. Omma. I am your son. It has taken me this long to write because I never knew what I would say, or I worried that it would be wrong, or bad, or ~~insuff~~ not good enough. But what more do I have to lose? The heartache it takes to write this? My heart is already broken. But it has somehow repaired. I think about your heart. I wonder how you think about me: a black night, a vast question, a difficult chapter, a hole, a loss, a moon.

I can't tell if I am writing this for me or for my daughter. I want her to have an idea for how to navigate her own black nights, her vast questions. Her road does not have to follow mine, but I want her to know she can act: shape, create, pray, move, read, write, draw, dance, sing, live. We have to live. ~~I am afraid I've forgotten why I want to write you.~~ I am afraid I've forgotten why I want to write you. I want to write to you to tell you that I love you. More than any other reason, I want that: to say I love you. You might read this and never want to speak to me, and I've made peace with that, a second leaving, another loss. But my desire to tell you that I love you is greater than my fear of another rejection, so I will say it again. I love you. Sarang hae, omma. Maybe I said that wrong.

~~Here are other things I hope. I hope you have had a good life. If you're reading this, you're alive, probably at least 65, and I should have written sooner, but there is a life we've lived. I want to know what you survived. I want you to know that I forgive you, that I think about you, that you have a granddaughter, a daughter-in-law, and and we are all creative and dreamers of sorts. My adoptive family was good to me, and I saw a lot of death here, or I should say I noticed a lot of death.~~ Do you want to meet? My heart is full and aching just thinking about meeting you. At this point in our lives, what could we do? I don't expect anything, but I hope for something. Tell me you're alive. Tell me you'll meet me. I know you might not. Tell me what you've never wanted to but have to so your own spirit will be free. I can handle any heartbreak you can imagine. I have prepared myself for 50 years. I have prepared myself for 50 years to hear nothing and to know that it means something, that I wrote this letter, that I sent it to you. I will write another version that is more traditional, more to the point, more about me, my life, and what I want from you. But I really want to send you this one. I want my daughter to know she is alive, beautiful inside and out, loved and loved so much. Daughter, you are beautiful inside and out, and you are loved and loved so much.

Korean Mother, I love you.

Lee

~~Lee~~

~~Lee Kwang Soo~~

~~Lee~~

Lee

Dear Korean Father,

~~I don't know what to say.~~ Abeoji. Appa. Do you know about me? Where do you live? I imagine you were a drinker. Or, an artist, a writer, an architect, or a wanderer with whom birth mother fell with one night, or maybe you were in love. Or you're reading this and thinking *my son has no clue*. You may be right, so I am writing this to make my own map. My chronology feels like this. If I was born in late 1970, and the Korean War ended in 1953, you must have been around 17-20 years old during the war. If you were older, then you lived through the war in your twenties or thirties, and so I am a war fracture. An artifact. A fact of war. Were you a poet? Have you looked for me? Probably not. But you had to have seen me. In a dream. In a store. In a story.

~~I should tell you about myself.~~
I live in California. ~~I would like to meet you.~~ I would like to hear the sound of your voice. I want to know you found peace, that you have a good life, that you are healthy. Or, if you are dying or dead, I want to know how you died. I hope this is not any bad wish. I want you to rest in peace. ~~You have rested in my mind more peacefully than one might think.~~ It's a strange absence, your voice, but somehow I can imagine your face more than birth mother's. I wonder if you ever kissed her. I pray there was no violence. I pray for all of us. I never prayed growing up, in a real sense. I didn't know I would need the grace of God. But I did, and I do. I have written a letter to mother three times: once as a child, once in Korea when I searched for her, and once last week before I wrote this. This is the first letter I have written to you. I hope it reaches you. But I've made my hard heart soft by forgiving myself, my birth country, birth mother, you. I forgive you. I love you. I love myself.

I am typing this from a beach house south of Santa Barbara. My wife and daughter are asleep, as I wake early and like to write before the day has begun. When my daughter wakes up, she will tell me *Happy Father's Day*. We might go for a walk on the beach. She's a brave girl. She's your granddaughter. In America, today is Father's Day. Happy Father's Day.

~~I love you.~~
~~Can I say that I love you?~~
I love you.
~~Lee Kwang Soo~~
Lee

# Erasure

My Asian body has been erased, muted, not drawn, or not considered in most education, media, business, political, creative, and corporate spheres. I didn't have an Asian American teacher until my junior year of college. I rarely saw Asians on television—except for *M\*A\*S\*H*, a show I never liked, a comedy set during the Korean War—that famous theme song's title is "Suicide Is Painless"—where the only Koreans you saw ran quietly in the background while the white doctors ogled Loretta Swift or mocked the only person of color on the show, Jamie Farr, who played the cross-dressing source of mockery. Margaret Cho's sitcom lasted for one season in 1994. *Fresh Off the Boat*, the first show in 20 years with an Asian American family, debuted in 2015. But growing up, I didn't see a lot of myself, and you probably didn't either. The American films I saw featured Bruce Lee, brilliant icon that he is, but in my youth, having been called his name by so many racist white kids, I learned to hate Bruce Lee until only recently. Other Asians were the sidekick, the nuclear threat, or the exoticized femme. In grade school, we learned about Martin Luther King Jr. for a day, as if that came anywhere near close to educating us about black culture, and we learned about Cesar Chavez, again, as if that covered Latinx history or culture. Maybe that was the point—it wasn't meant to cover it, but rather, to cover themselves, to absolve the school, the board, the administration, and anyone else of any wrongdoing when it came to omissions, who needed to placate a growing number of people who demanded a broader education. As for Asian history or culture? Forget it. I don't remember learning about any Asian American activists—Helen Zia, Grace Lee Boggs, Yuri Kochiyama. Filmmakers like Lee Chang Dong, Park Chan Woo, Bong Joon Ho. There were none, as far as my education would have it. Wait. No. I learned how Japan attacked the U.S. in World War II. Despite every erasure and absence, every silence and mockery, people like me were not only present but we were important: our stories matter. Despite what microaggressions or violences against us may exist, my body is now being drawn, considered, and noticed. As I piece something together the resembles my body in this country, I know we are more than a Zen garden. We are more than robot, math whiz, karate kid. We are not evil nor empire.

# Koreanness

*"I am from there. I am from here.*
*I am not there and I am not here.*
*I have two names, which meet and part,*
*and I have two languages.*
*I forget which of them I dream in."*


— Mahmoud Darwish


To know my Korean-ness, I had to know my Whiteness. To know my Whiteness, I had to know my Korean-ness. In Amy Tan's essay, "Mother Tongue," Tan writes about being ashamed of her Mother's English when she was a young girl with excellent English. At age eight, she pretended to be her mother on the phone with a banker, who felt it easier to talk to an eight year-old with no accent rather than a grown woman with an Asian one. Language is a significant marker for the Asian American community, and it marks most Asians' experiences of difference in the United States, where they number over 20 million and comprise 5.6 per cent of the population (37% if you're in Hawaii, 14% if you're in California, near 10% in New Jersey, New York, and Washington).

In my home, Whiteness. My White family wouldn't notice it, just as fish would struggle to explain water, or humans would struggle to explain air. My father, Newbold Herrick III, yes, that's right—Newbold the third— was from New York originally. His father was in finance, and his mother, who lived to be 96, was a nurse, and then for as long as I can remember, a charitable and whip-smart woman. She graduated from Smith College in the 1930s with a degree in physics. She was an early feminist. Her grandson would be Korean. In the 1950s, she moved to Ojai, California, where she made a life and had a real influence on the community. Her father, my great-grandfather Sherman Day Thacher, founded the Thacher School, a boarding high school nestled in the Topa Topa mountains. My paternal great-grandfather went to Yale, and my paternal grandfather went to Yale. My father went to boarding school and was reared in this affluent lifestyle, although the boarding school experience ended with him, as I attended public schools. My parents asked me if I would like to attend Midland, another boarding school in Los Olivos, California, where my father went and where his brother taught for several decades. But this world was foreign to me.

Once, around 1980, when my mom's fatigue hit a climax and she tired of our dirty shoes, one day she made a large white sign and taped it to the door that said, "Stop! Take off your shoes!" This was her way of reminding Holly and me to do just that, but I liked it because it was an Asian tradition to take off one's shoes in the house. I loved taking my shoes off.

For Thanksgiving, not Chuseok, we had turkey, mashed potatoes, my mom's famous stuffing with healthy portions of sausage, cranberry sauce, green beans and a salad, and rolls. Bread. Whiteness. No rice, no noodles, no chopsticks, no gojuchang. No makkolei, no soju, no Hite. I didn't even learn to use chopsticks until my 20s. I was raised White, and so I know what it means. It means traditions, family, and love. But in my middle to upper class family, it also meant a world of privilege. (This is important: white privilege is not connected to merely financial advantages; it is the privilege of *not having to care* about racism. But I digress). We lived in a more affluent part of Modesto called Del Rio, a block away from a private country club with a world-class 18-hole golf course. We had a cabin that my father and grandfather built in a tiny town called Mosquito in Placerville County. And the beach house.

The beach house is a two-bedroom, two-bathroom cottage on the coast of Carpinteria, California, ten minutes south of Santa Barbara. My great-grandmother built it in 1938—the first house at Rincon Point, a world-renowned surf spot known for its long break. Kevin Costner had a home there. It's minutes from where Oprah Winfrey, Ellen DeGenres, Conan O'Brien, and George Lucas have homes. But I know it as a second home, a small, rustic beach house that looks out into the wide, blue Pacific Ocean. My privilege was real. But as much as I benefitted from it, I also never felt comfortable with it, probably because I never fully experienced it. Whereas I felt at home on that beach, walking amidst the comfortable California beach-house owners, I rarely looked like home to others.

Whiteness meant being insulated from what I grew to experience and feel on a visceral, daily basis. Racism micro-aggressions, othered. Once, at a gas station in Turlock, where I attended college, a woman angrily called me *damn Jap* because I pulled in to pump gas as she was about to pull out and leave. It was the first time I encountered what many White people believe is their privilege: public space and their right to it. I can't begin to count how many times a white person—and in *my* experience, it is almost always a white woman, for some reason—insists that I am in the way, in their space, not in my place, which in their minds is quietly and submissively out of mind. Not to be bothered. Not to move or give way. Not to be watched in a store or pulled over by the police, randomly. To be free to move freely and unfettered. To be unmoved by the state's violence against people of color, and thus, dismayed or irritated by those victim's anger, protests, requests, or signs that they matter.

It could be an American sensibility. The perceived right to the land, the gold, the laws. The historical amnesia, the plausible deniability. What Native genocide? What Chinese exclusion? What slavery? What laws prohibiting people of color from filing claims to gold they found in California in 1849 and 1850? What atomic bombs on Hiroshima and Nagasaki? What Japanese American internment? What Vincent Chin? What Eric Garner? What Fong Lee? What detention centers, with children in cages?

# Stars

Every now and then, I remember that I was born on the other side of the earth, and it makes sense that I love looking up at the stars. It's such a childish thing to do, like climbing trees, stomping in puddles, and building forts out of blankets. But there's some strange pull and a simple satisfaction from looking at the stars after all these years. I wonder if a man my age in Korea has the same love. I wonder how the stars relate to a gravitational likelihood that I'll tell my daughter someday about the time in our backyard, swimming in the moonlight, and the world seemed perfect. Or the time I dropped her off at her middle school in Fresno, and before I drove off, she motioned for me to stop, fogged up the window with her breath, and wrote with her finger, "I love you, Dad" with a heart, and the world seemed perfect. That's what it is about the stars. Because they're so many millions of miles away and so still, the immediate chaos or confusion of our lives seems so minor. Even in the daylight, they're right there. Imperceptible but there. Something like faith, or belief, or the wild idea that a deep kind of joy is there for you, even if you have no idea where it is.

Lee becomes a citizen of the United States.
Naturalization ceremony, California, May 1975.
Courtesy of the Author.

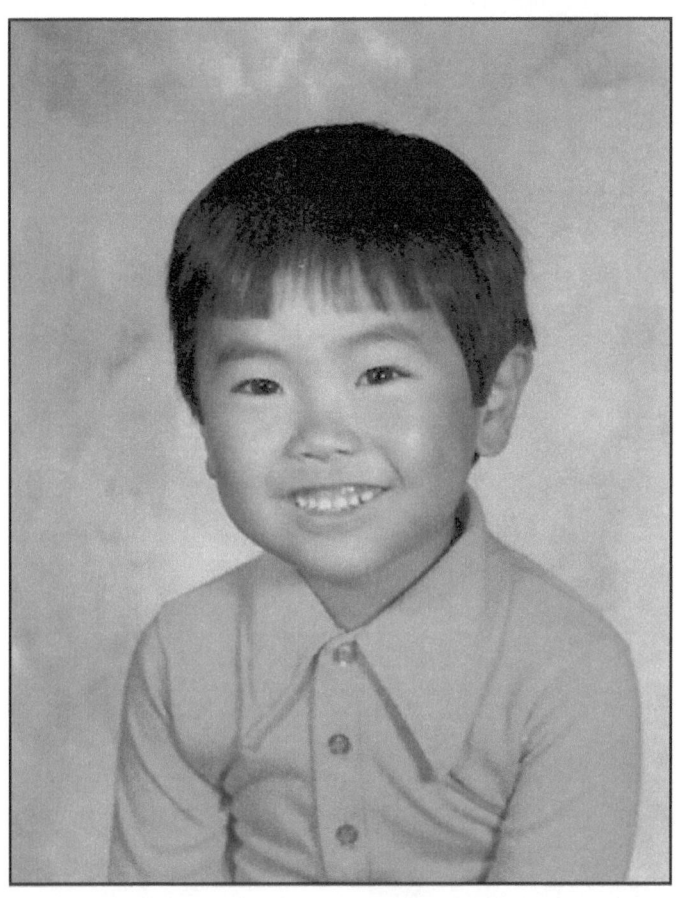

Lee in kindergarten, Danville, California, 1976.
Courtesy of the Author.

NEW POEMS, 2020-2024

## In Praise of Late Wonder

I've wondered what my Korean mother's voice
sounded like when I was born. Was it gasp, hiss,
or flag in light wind? I've wondered if she kissed
me before I became a wind, a white noise
in blue sky. I've wondered lately about joy.
Butterfly, hummingbird, angels so full of bliss
they almost sing. I imagine some of this
relates to the orphan I was, the adopted boys
and girls like me, all diaspora and alarm.
I've wondered if I'm made of smoke and fire.
Sometimes, clear sky. Sometimes, quiet storm.
I've wondered lately how the acoustic guitar
keeps its secrets, makes me float a little higher.
How could I not love looking at the stars?

## The Time I Spent Inside a Star

How could I not love looking at the stars?
Once, I dreamt that I climbed inside of one.
It was darker than you'd think, but still fun
enough to feel like astronomy. There was a bar
serving drinks mixed with cosmic dust, bizarre
but delicious. It felt like a kind of heaven,
like I imagine California or Daejeon.
I want to read my birth mother's memoir.
To remember is an attempt to be free.
The time I spent inside a star,
I've wondered how to best believe
it was real. It was no more a dream
than I am alive and have made it this far,
dust-covered, full of joy, evergreen.

# Partial Crown in Praise of Absent Sounds

I want the fax machine, the dot matrix
buzz saw of news across the wire,
the young woman's lisp and fire
during solo moonlight road trips,
the shuffle of predictable card tricks,
the acoustic chord like sweet desire,
the rotary dial and pronunciation error.
When I say absent sounds, I mean
typewriter key as much as aniyo or ye,
the 8-track plunk as much as Korean
vowels drawn out at the end like a plain
blue sky. I want to know the way
home. There's not much more I need.

Home. There's not much more I need
except to know how much blue sky
there is from here to you, why
I sometimes hear your voice freed,
wild, true. Please, take the lead.
At times, I thought I was going to die.
At times, fire. At other times, firefly.
My daughter was four at the art gallery
and called it the art galaxy, a malapropism
I wish existed: star, sonnet, serenade.
I want the mispronunciation, broken rhythm
and scratched record. Survivor wisdom.
A mother's prayer for her son, who stayed
perfectly still when she left and kissed him.

# Abecedarian Love Song for Street Food

*"Street food, I believe, is the salvation of the human race."*
—Anthony Bourdain

All praise for the pozole glistening in midday light
by the grace of the woman near the comal. In southern
California, Raul Martinez unveiled a mobile
downtown goldmine of al pastor by a bar in
East LA for the drunk, the artists, the necessary
future waiting in line. Praise be to the ice cream truck,
glory of the van's slow roll, so praise the van,
hut, cart, booth, tent, stall, stand, bike, or truck.
I once devoured a tlayuda in Oaxaca City, broke down
just as the sunlight burst through the heart of a woman
kissing her baby's forehead by the plaza. When I say
love, what I mean to say is I dream of you through disaster,
malady, drought, or this nightmare anxiety pandemic.
Now, even in this late dying, let us praise the 20,000
open-hearted vendors in Bangkok and the glorious
pupusas in San Salvador I ate on a bench near a dove.
Quesadilla. Arepa. Tteokbokki. Hallelujah. The banh mi
right on the outskirts of Hue, the chili pepper, the cilantro
songs, praise the Zocalo saints who brought me
to tears with a taco so full of music I almost wept.
Under the Beijing moonlight, bao zi is made by angels,
vendors with wings if you know where to look. On
West 53rd and 6th Ave, NYC, halal, or in Fresno, no
xenophobe is welcome. Tell me what to eat—
your chuan, your eloté, your mouthful of pure
zen, like savory, surprising flashes of heaven.

# Acclimation

My first language was the ocean.
It sounded like my first mother's
body: wave, storm, vanish.

I love what the wind does
to the trees. I want nature
to move me like that.

My name is a song. In it,
there are horses, fed by a man
who says I feel American when I kill

a row of ants and say they asked for it.
We are this many miles from desire.
We are immigrant turned imperialist.

I love what the wind does to the bay.
Wave to me. Smile at me
like you know my name,

like you love the ocean, too,
or at least the way
I glisten in the starlight.

# Poem for the Families of Chávez Ravine

*After Vincent Valdez and Ry Cooder,* El Chávez Ravine, *oil painting on a 1953 ice cream truck, portraying the forced removal of predominantly Mexican American families for the construction of Dodger Stadium*

*I remember looking at my house. My mother was already all broken. My father built that house. I was born there. It had a vine growing, and it covered all the roof in the front. In spring, it looked like it was wearing a white crown.*

—Cenovia Gamboa, Chávez Ravine resident as a young girl

In the angelic city, a boxer prepares
to jab while the dogs roam free
under the telephone wires.
Home is where my heart was,
white crown of flowers,
Lalo Guerrero on the record player,
the gold sun over the canyon,
homes on a hill before the land study,
before forced removal, before the bulldozers,
before the development that never developed,
before a woman who most fiercely wanted
to stay was carried off by men with guns,
before the Dodgers.

We'll cheer on the team.
We like baseball, but not this way, not on the land
where home became home plate in the new stadium.
See the field of freshly mowed grass?
You see outfield. I see corn field.
You say luxury boxes. I see mailboxes.

*This letter is to inform you that a public housing*
*development will be built on this location for families*
*of low income.* What we mean to say is
your home will be destroyed.
*It will be several months before your property*
*is purchased. Later you will have the first chance*
*to move back into the new Elysian Heights Park development.*
What we mean to say is that the development
will never be built but the land will be sold
for a fraction to a baseball team owner and
your home will be destroyed.
This vagueness of the language is not accidental.
When is later? What is a chance?
What is development in the face of displacement?
What angels watched? What angels remember?
What kind of new grace should we build?

## Library Sonnet

I am looking for a good book
where I can find part of myself I need
to discover, where I can get lost, read,
explore, escape. Robots, recipes, rookies
who made it big. Once, I took
home a story that made me feel alive, free,
new. I returned it (on time—no late fee)
and couldn't stop dreaming for weeks.
Anytime, anywhere, I am at home in a library.
There is hope and help shelved next to the joy.
Whatever your questions or emotions—weary,
needful, ready for inspiration, something scary—
The poetry! The stories! They say, please, enjoy
this light, for you, this world of possibility.

# Ten Statements for the Committee

1. If I were to believe my education and my media,
   I was erasure after erasure
   until I was almost erased.

2. I feel American listening to A Tribe Called Quest
   or Yeah Yeah Yeahs more than any
   Bruce Springsteen song.

3. That is to say birthright, that is to say imperial,
   that is to say, violence and coup is when I feel
   sadness filling up my mouth.

4. I'm tired of Hollywood white heroism.

5. In my Hollywood, it so happens the main character
   can be two things at once: Asian and heroic.

6. I've seen thousands of brown people saving the day.

7. I was born in Korea and adapted.

8. What we need, we've always had: the museums inside of us.

9. In the end, farmers and librarians will save us.

10. Meet me in the field or the library. I'll wait for you.

# The Birds Outside My Window Sing During a Pandemic

What we need has always been inside of us.
For some—a few poets or farmers, perhaps—
it's always near the surface. Others, it's buried.
It was in our original design, though—pre-machine,
pre-border, pre-pandemic. I imagine it like the light
one might feel through the body before dying,
a warm calm, a slow breath, a sweet rush.
There is, by every measure, reason for fear,
concern, a concert in the balcony of anxiety
made of what has also always been inside of us:
a kind of knowing that everything could break.
But it hasn't quite yet and probably won't.
What I mean to say is, I had a day dream
and got lost inside of it. There were dozens
of birds for some reason, who sounded like
they were singing in different accents:
*shelter in place, shelter in place.*
*You're made of stars and grace.*
*Stars and grace. Stars and grace.*

*From* S*CAR AND* F*LOWER* (2019)

Dear _____,

When you lost me, or when your heart caved,
or when your heart flew through the city like wild herons
on the ledge of my broken window sill in another country,
you name infinity as the home of your intoxication,
ferment as the placeholder for love, the ocean sized grace
of our common language, the ocean sized chance in this
moment. Grace. That's what I meant to tell you about.
I saw it a few times in my life. I saw my daughter cradle
the broken body of a tiny bird. I saw a young poet
repair the broken charm of a younger poet. I saw that
poet forgive another poet by a stream in the City of God,
by a monument for mothers like you who write poems
about men like me, who write by the ocean with their dogs
waking in the morning cool, the wild seabirds searching
the waves for a small fish to devour.

## What I Hear After the Massacre
## and What I Mistake for My Heart

Invisible birds shocked out of the trees
and you mistake them for children
on the playground, or you mistake the leaves
cracked underfoot for the children's hush
or broken glass.  It's a maelstrom.
At the Winter Program, the second graders
sing "Let It Snow" and the parents clasp
their hands, half exhale, half prayer.
The children sing in your town and you
think of the children in the shattered town.
All that comes to you is their hearts, heaven,
hell, and the next kind word you will say to a boy.

# What I Hear When I Hear You in My Head

is the little whisper, the aggregate sorrow, the father's
heavy weeping as the son's heavy weeping. What I hear
is your artistic response after the massacre, the family
of clasped hands, Black hands, Brown hands, a small child
whose brother never had a chance, who holds her father's
tearful face and says, "Your eyes are like the moon," is
what I hear when I hear you in my head this evening,
your laughter like tiny harps. I hear your fatigue as
another way to say: deprivation. I hear recount, re-tally,
a retaliation is what I hear when I hear you in my head
is the grace, the charm, the dead, the boy, the dead boy,
the boy who died because of the fear, the forest in
the other man's heart, the gun, the heartbreak is the sound
I hear when I hear you in my head is how we each sigh
with distinction, where fatigue meets fire, where we wake
and wonder: if we all go out to a field tonight, sit by a fire,
say the most honest thing you have ever said in your life,
would any dead boy or girl reappear, not like a mirage
but reappear, not like a voice in my head but a body
in this room, with flesh and bones, with his big smile,
orange blossoms in his billowing hair?

## I Got a Letter from the Government the Other Day

I watched my hands turn into flags,

waving at the top of a government building before the bombs,

I watched books about fat content burn on the crosswalk

where a dead pigeon splayed out like a Banksy

where the drunk poets walked to the café

to haggle over Whitman's place in the canon

this is so far from any large-scale weaponry

most kids could care less about revolution or poetry

but revolution has everything to do with the fire

lit in the girl whose father read to her

so that when she is fully grown and the bombs

detonate on her city's bridges she will know

the perfect epigraph to rally the women

who know where the wood and the matches await.

# Fatigue

The mother cries into her black tea.
The mother weeds in the small yard.

The father cries into his old tea,
tries to bring his son back to life, wonders

why again, why the gun, why the cop,
why the fire, where's the rain,

why the gun, why the gun,
why the hole, in the head, in the dream

why theater, why the school grounds,
why headline, why sonnet,

why ammunition, why the acquittal,
why the killer can't hear the doves

why the boy cannot run with a hood
why some men craft hate with theirs

why again, why the gun, why the cop
where's the out, where's the cry

why the tie, why the tale,
why the black, why the brown,

why again, why we die,
why the sun goes down like this.

# Rose

*At the New York Botanical Garden, for the 49 killed and 53 wounded
at the Pulse Nightclub shooting in Orlando*

This sudden desire to bloom, near
the astonishing splendor of the swamp,
there you are, unexpected and delivered
grace, rose and botany, petal and lure.
When the tourists leave, tell me
if you get tired. Why are you the Queen?
In another country, you are not royalty.
Tell me, rose, about root, soil, wilt.
I'm stealing a petal, and I know it's a crime.
I want the petal to fly from this botanical
garden to Orlando, where I cannot place a rose
on any altar but where I imagine forty-nine roses
near a swamp in a park, where even small children
know, don't terrorize the birds! Let no person deliver
terror in a park, in a school, in a dance club, no
terror in a dance club. I want to be quiet.
The roses admit they don't know why they bloom.
But they do. The rose, its pulse, doing its loveliness
in a time of disaster, dancing like the world was on fire.

# Repertoire

The nastiest lick in the whole damn repertoire
is in the first movement, the conductor said
to the first violin. A concerto like tonight's is
a dream swell, a dark circus of fluted magic,
the nasty hell of your own difficult year,
the bright chorus of your own survival, awash
in a floral weave of ocean foam among the dreaming
musicians preparing for the nasty lick, their lips
tightened like fists, rusted knives in a deep inventory:
one blade for large game, one blade for short trees,
one blade for berries, one blade for gutting the whole
damn idea. We have, what the conductor would call
a repertoire: how to maneuver if you aren't in tune,
how to bail when the wave overtakes you, when
the concerto has such mean licks you almost break,
the lights dizzy the fighter in you, but your repertoire
comes back to you in some animal moment, your breath
now in time with your instrument, and everything
aligns as it should: your glistening body healed from
the incision, your flawed key buried under your shining
knives, your favorite chapter, your go-to song.

## Exile

Our natural
state is not

defensive
or tense

but water
in a resting

state.
We state this

to be true
in an age

of inquiry,
our failure

to put what
is just

before
ease. There

are lovers in
another country

reclining by
a fire, admitting

love in
a common language

with faith
in the exiles

of their state,
where

a woman
looks at her friend

and says
please, put down

your bag
and stay.

Please, stay
to see how

the movie ends.
Take my hand.

I think the city
might go

up
in flames.

## Stray Light

Oh Lady Mercy,
our country of auction block

and cracked teeth
under the steel toed boot,

how easy our dismissal
because the game is on.

Say the robots
learned to love

by the time I discovered my body,
fireflies organized

the stray light,
harnessed it for energy

in small villages
for dreaming women.

The men listened
to the elders report by the fire light:

if you gather the data
from your heartbreak

you'll find it's just dust now.
It is not too late for discovery.

It is not too late to learn the radius
of past despair.

The children forget
about maps,

never knew they existed,
so they lost the art of getting lost,

of being
lost, of feeling loss.

If it were only shock,
the after-shock of your spine tremble,

if it were only about waves: water,
electrical, sound, the slow rumble

you know by now,
we would walk around

with our dumb mouths
open in awe,

not because we are dumb
but because a father cradles a dying

stranger with his left leg gone,
with metal shrapnel peppered

into the side of his face, near
his cheekbones, where the stranger,

a boy, touches the man's
face and learns the importance

of human touch
in the minutes before dying.

## Testimony

I heard the American poet groan
like his farmworker mother bent
into California's central question
like a rake or a comma or a death
that was not a death but a rising
fire or a shotgun in a wheat field.

I heard the father say to himself
*to hell with it* before he wrote
a seven-page manifesto on the crimes
of lemon trees whose leaves become
little whispers in our dream like
yellow flowers floating on a lake.

I heard anger come into the night
I head the night bring you down
I heard the down say please madam
I heard a woman say Hmong means free
I heard freedom like kingdom.

# Firefly

I wrote her name in the sand
with the tiny parade of fireflies

flitting above my head
and it came true,

a nearly black night
lit with bright yellow question

marks, little fires you
thought would break you

but never did, not even
the long year of paralysis.

When you write your
daughter's name in the sand

it is permanent, even as the water
washes it away, you

have done it—that was the act,
the action, permanent as fire.

Revolution

The revolution broke out
in your very own heart.
Your heart a hundred
flaming questions.
The daughters' strong
arms, a bounty, a blue sky
melting down every semi-
automatic. What guns ever
eased a grandmother's trauma?
The revolution broke out in riots.
It was all women and girls.
They taught me how to say guerra.
She said the city is in my heart.
She said Oaxaca, Chiapas,
Teotihuacan. Chichicastenango,
Tegucigalpa, San Salvador.
She said my name is Hue, Seoul,
Qingdao. Guangzhou. Luong
Prabang, Phnom Penh,
Kingston, Chiang Mai,
Mumbai, Manila, Havana,
Tehran, Shiraz, Mosul,
Fallujah, Mukalla, Rafah,
Mogadishu, Kyoto, Aleppo,
Fresno. The girl on fire
inside my heart said don't
forget the woman's hands,
the arms, her ocean sized
heart, aunt's molcajete,
her sister's papaya salad.

She said, measure the capacity
of your chest, what valves
and caves to excavate.
She said, tonight, let us
do what the heart teaches
us, how it breaks us open
and shakes us clean.
Protect it. How the world
is a story—the afternoon
sunlight in a girl's black hair,
the fine lines in a woman's
small hands, the dreams
they share by the fire.

# Erasure

When I was boy and the moon
had not yet occurred to me, my name
given to me by an American couple full of grief
and readiness, I sinned by cursing my mother.
How could I know I would need the moon?
I wished bad things for her because she cared
hard that I would make it. I cursed her because
I knew the shape of her hand, a porcelain shell
lighter than mine, and I could not form the words
to curse anyone else. Every now and then,
I remember that I was born on the other side
of the world, and it makes sense that I love
looking at the stars, such a foolish thing to do
as a grown man, or such an important thing to do
as a grown man, my brown body glistening
in the pool, starlight flashing in my wet black hair.

# Elegy

*For Phillip Clay (1974-2017) — born in South Korea adopted to the United States, deported back to Korea, committed suicide in 2017*

In my dream, when you fell through
the sky from fourteen stories high,
all burning paper, your body broke
into a hundred flowers and floated
into the clouds. The moon and stars: still.
Your fire now ash, your spirit free, wild,
and true in a deep calm, where country
is a black night, a blank question
of insufficient starlight, where no child,
man or woman, no idea as beautiful as you
is ever deported, is ever only the harsh light
of your deepest wound. I wish I could have
eaten your fire and howled with you:
eclipse, fracture, angelic cloud song.
May the wild and broken stars remember you.
May you be at peace in a quiet part of the sky.

## How Music Stays in the Body

Your body is a song called birth
or first mother, a miracle that gave birth
to another exquisite song. One song raises
three boys with a white husband. One song
fought an American war overseas. One song leapt
from fourteen stories high, and like a dead bird,
shattered into the clouds. Most forgot the lyrics
to their own bodies or decided to paint abstracts
of mountains or moons in the shape of your face.
I've been told Mothers don't forget the body.
I can't remember your face, the shape or story,
or how you held me the day I was born, so
I wrote one thousand poems to survive.
I want to sing with you in an open field,
a simple room, or a quiet bar. I want to hear
your opinions about angels. Truth is, angels drink,
too—soju spilled on the halo, white wings sticky
with gin, as if any mother could forget the music
that left her. You should hear how loudly I sing
now. I've become a ballad of wild dreams and coping
mechanisms. I can breathe now through any fire.
I imagine I got this from him or you, my earthly
inheritance: your arms, your sigh, your heavy song.
I know all the lyrics. I know all the blood.
I know why angels howl into the moonlight.

# Manifesto

I wanted to write a manifesto
about the ocean,

a treatise on the wild trees'
outlandish demands,

alone under moonlight
translating my name:

dreamer, ascendant,
question.

My Korean name
means bright light,

what appears after
despair,

how you write Korean
instead of Koran

and think
of your friend

who worked Gibran
into his wedding

vows, how
love is the water

between two beaches,
one a country

where your name was
Lee Kwang Soo,

one a country
where you are renamed

Lee Herrick, and you are
what you always

were, a question,
a bruised persimmon,

a dreamer
imagining the revolt.

# Breath

## 1.

By the time I discovered my body
it was perfectly human, all this sin,
the chambers and aorta of the large muscle,
I was a series of numbers on a chart,
the start of the mouth

## 2.

If you gather the data
from the robots of your city
the wires all shine
in certain light and the kids
inhale a canopy of polluted air
heave a last prayer

## 3.

We call the body, heart
calls the body, the body calls the hurt
natural, we call nature a tree on fire
from only heat, its own burn

## 4.

We call this idea: agriculture,
poetry culture
or office culture:
the sum, the atoms. What you take
in before you let breath out.

## Lecture

I came to hear
the painter talk

about sunlight
in Paris but herons

broke out
of the tiny lecture hall.

The painter caught one
with her bare hand

as it sprung. This,
she claimed, was joyful

equal to anything
she could say

about the influence of light
in Lima on her work.

We felt the light
in the room like the light

in the herons' pale feathers
that became the painters'

dark pastels, the bruises
of her next wild idea.

# Flight

The in-flight magazine crossword partially done,
a corner begun here, scratched out answers there,
one set of answers in pencil, another in the green.
The woman with the green ball point knew
the all-time hit king is Rose and the Siem Reap
treasure is Angkor Wat. The woman, perhaps
en route to hold her dying mother's hand in Seattle,
forgot about death for ten minutes while remembering
her husband's Cincinnati Reds hat while gardening after
the diagnosis. Her handwriting was so clean. Maybe
she was a surgeon. Maybe a painter. No. What painter
wouldn't know 17 down, Diego's love, five letters?
In a rush, her dying mother's voice came back
to her, or maybe she was a Chinese adoptee
and her first mother's imagined voice said, wo ai ni.
At 30,000 feet, you focus on 33 across, Asian
American classic, *The Woman* _____,
when a stranger in the window seat sees the clue,
watches me write in W, and she says *Warrior*.
and for a moment you forget it is your favorite memoir,
and she reminds you of lilies or roses, Van Gogh
or stems with thorns, art galleries in romantic cities
where she is headed but you should not go. The flight
attendant grazes my shoulder. The crossword squares,
the letters, the chairs and aisles seem so tight in flight,
but there is nothing here but room, really.
Maybe the next passenger will know
what I do not: 64 down, five letters, Purpose.
And why do we remember what we do? We know
the buzz of Dickinson's fly and the number of years

in Marquez's solitude, but some things we will never
know, as it should be: why the body sometimes rumbles
like a plane hurtling over southern Oregon, how
exactly we fall in love, or if Frida and Maxine
Hong Kingston would have loved the same kind of tea.

# Echolocation

What a miracle it would be
to echolocate like a bat,

to shriek and have the shriek
bounce back to alert us

to the oncoming train, the wrong person,
or a year of trouble.

The organism which hears best
is the Greater Wax Moth,

which can hear 100 kHz more
than the bat, which preys on the moth.

And what do we hear, with poor night
vision and no ability for flight?

Can you hear your lover hum near the stove?
You are one of many species who can whistle.

Pigeons hear lower frequencies
and can detect coming storms.

Dogs can differentiate between their owners'
footsteps and a stranger's.

And what have you heard tonight,
the low sigh of your father's fatigue,

the scrape of a brush on the canvas,
the echo of your singular breathing.

# Truths

*"Some things you know all your life. They are so simple and true,*
*they must be said without elegance."*
                    —Philip Levine

I will say it like this: I watched my daughter bite into a peach,
and although she did not have the language for it yet,
I imagined her thinking, that taste, that perfect juice,
is heavenly. There was a certain light in Fresno that day,
like today, where we work, and dream—
Mayor and mothers, farmers and fathers, laborers
in blue collars and donors for the red wave,
one city of multiple truths straight down the 99
dreaming about the perfect peach, the perfect pitch,
one city in the shape of an immigrant's beautiful accent,
one city of taco, gyro, pan dulce, and strawberries
so good, you'd swear they came straight from the hand of God,
one city, in my dream, where there are no gunshots tonight
or the next one hundred starlit nights, one simple truth
called the fig tree, the ash tree, one poet's testimony
stripped of its elegance for the city to consider:
in which of our ninety languages should I say that I love you?
Which of our two hundred and fifty different crops would you like
to taste, to imagine its perfect juice? My truths involve dreams,
stars, hard work and good pay for the ice worker, the tractor
driver, the backyard gardener, the students and the teachers,
the nurses and the preachers. The fog on a country road—
that is the truth. Our menacing heat in July—truth.
My city is your city, a bead of sweat and the will
to work, the want for clean air, for water,
for a moment of grace in the shade.

# Strawberries

I pulled into the dirt lot for delicious strawberry
because I stop for entrepreneurs and grammar like that.
What is more American? I too came from another country,
like someone once did in your family, who had what it took
to farm in a new language, learn the laws, learn the people.
When I was a boy before I became a citizen,
I pledged allegiance to the flag before I knew
what allegiance was, what an ally was, what a republic was, or
what it meant to stand. I entered the dream of the farmer
when I walked up to his business, each basket
of berries another dollar for his son who has not been
to Southeast Asia but knows California well, knows
the supermarkets and the malls, the ocean swells
and the angle of sunlight in his mother's fatigue.
The farmer speaks like a poet, dreaming about the river
back home. I bet his favorite American poet would be Rich
or Whitman, Espada or Vang. I buy six baskets and no sky opens,
no doves break into flight but the first perfect strawberry
glistens in the valley light before I take it into my mouth
and become a citizen of these open American fields.

Prayers

Imagine you are
the last line in this
poem somewhere
in a desert with no
data or comment
threads, only the creek
water light as a cloud,
in the sand
where plants quit.
You will wait
for the information:
map, verdict, prayer,
so be grateful, lovers,
be kind, children,
and the whole blanket
of stars will shake
out and settle like
tiny silver prayers
in your hair.

# Anechoic

George Foy stayed in the anechoic chamber
for 45 minutes and nearly went mad.
He could hear the blood rushing in
his veins and began to wonder if he was
hallucinating. He had been to a monastery,
an American Indian sweat lodge,
and a nickel mine two kilometers underground.
In the anechoic chamber, the floor's design
eliminates the sound of footsteps.
NASA trains astronauts in anechoic chambers
to cope with the silence of space.
Without echo, in the quietest place on earth,
what else can we hold onto? What replaces sound
in concert with what you see? The human voice,
the timber when a person says kamsahamnida
or yes, please, or fuerte, is 25 to 35 decibels.
Hearing damage can start around 115 decibels.
Metallica, front row, possible damage
albeit possible love. The Who, 126 decibels.
A Boeing Jet, 165 decibels. The whale, low rumble
frequency and all, 188 decibels, can be heard
for hundreds of miles underwater.
I once walked around inside a whale heart,
which is the size of a small car. The sound
was like Brian Doyle's heart that gave out
at 60 after he wrote my favorite essay
about the joyas voladoras and the humming
bird heart, the whale heart, and the human
heart. Glass can break at 163 decibels.
Hearing is the last sense to leave us.

Some say that upon death, our vision,
our taste, our touch, and our smell
might leave us, but some have been
pronounced dead and by all indication
are, but they can hear. In this moment,
when the doctor pronounces the time
or when the handgun pumps once more,
what light arrives? What sounds, the angels?
The Ultrasonic Weapon is used for crowd
control or to combat riots—as too many
humans gathered in one place for a unified
purpose can threaten the state. The state
permits gatherings if the flag waves. Sound
can be weaponized or made into art.
It can kill. It can heal a wound. It is
a navigation device and can help determine
if the woman has a second heart inside of her
now, the beating heart of a baby on the ultrasound,
a boy or a girl, making a new music in the body
of another body, a chorus, a concert, a hush.

# Sun

*The sun, with all those planets revolving around it and dependent on it, can still ripen a bunch of grapes as if it had nothing else in the universe to do.*
—Galileo

When I was a boy, and the moon had not yet occurred to me,
the astronomy of my body was simple and true.
I was all sun, all heat, all brown adoption high on fire.
I got lost in a forest I thought was an ocean.
My sister knew it was a lake but let me figure it out.
I saw the lilies, the dying, the heartbreak to come.
So I came to the idea that I would not die
before I spent a full night staring up at the moon
before I wrote a poem near Teotihuacan,
before I returned to the city in which I became an erasure
before the other side of planet becomes home,
the California poppies in the front yard, the grape
vines in full regalia with their questions
exploding right there on the branch.

## Stay

I am not what you thought
an ocean would look like,
but once a fire starts in you,
there will always be ash.
There are long walks, thank
goodness, there are woods
to be small in, there are
anchors to the world so
you will not fly away before
it is time. The miracle of grass,
even though you may forget it,
the fact that you are loved,
even though you may forget it,
and what a miracle that is—
being loved—or more so,
that you are a wide blue ocean
capable of loving, you churning
body of sea life who survived
the oil spills, the broken glass,
the dead birds floating in the bay.

# Bathe

Some acts require the whole
body's attention,

how a light song fills
the auditorium.

Little bath wave over arm,
kite over wine,

on your back
in a porcelain heart.

Tiny flowers
near your head so moist

you could almost live there,
the city crashing

around your hips,
the artists remembering

the maps
to their deep root,

all the ache washed
out,

all the wine
slipping down the throat.

# Stars

Every now and then, I remember I was born

on the other side of the world, and it makes sense

that I love looking at the stars:

Little Apocalypse, The Human Condition,

The Bell Tribe, clusters I name above the field

where I kissed a woman with hair like black gold.

When Van Gogh looked out his asylum room

window and painted "Starry Night," the stars

above his country went blank for an instant—you

wouldn't have noticed—his hands all flurry and oils,

energy and devour, like fire, here a moon

with feathery wings, there a spangled crush of cloud.

In his eyes, the stars like madness.

In the stars, your country and silver shots of light.

In the window, your best self, your super nova,

your midnight prayer about dying.

# The House is Quiet, Except

my daughter reads on the couch,
whispers the dialogue. I only hear

the consonants of her name, the way

I imagine a house of books
in a future age,

2035, when I will be 65 and alive,

I hope, and she will be 31,
perhaps with faith and a love

she can count on—wild trees,

wild flowers, a man, or a woman.
Perhaps God or someone else

to whom she can whisper dialogue
if she forgets where her heart is,

how there is a pulse in every book,

how looking down into the open page
reminds us of prayer,

the next night of restoration,
the light around her body.

*From* GARDENING SECRETS OF THE DEAD (2012)

# Korean Poet in California

I am one of the war fractures—
a breathing fact of art,

the artifice, the brass hiss
from Isang Yun's first exiled concerto—

touch my arms and you will know.

# Gardening Secrets of the Dead

When the light pivots, hum—not so loud
the basil will know, but enough
to water it with your breath.
Gardening has nothing to do with names
like *lily* or *daisy*. It is about verbs like *uproot*,
*traverse*, *hush*. We can say it has aspects of memory
and prayer, but mostly it is about refraction and absence,
the dead long gone when the plant goes in. A part of the body.
Water and movement, attention and dirt.

       Once, I swam off the coast of Belize and pulled
seven local kids along in the shallow Caribbean,
their brown bodies in the blue water behind me,
the first one holding my left hand like a root,
the last one dangling his arm under the water
like a lavender twig or a flag in light wind.
A dead woman told me: gardening,
simply, is laughing and swimming
a chorus of little brown miracles
in water so clear you can see yourself
and your own brown hands becoming clean.

# Spectral Questions of the Body

When I imagine my birth mother's body, spectral
questions float: how the cage
of bone protects the heart, how she sounded
near death once or if bird cried
a song near the river. I imagine it like gel
in a body of water, a jellyfish in the sea,
a gasping squid.
                                If I could touch the body,
I would go for the neck
where air meets air, despair swapped for light
flashes, cusps of cut lavender,
cups of the silkworms you may have loved,
the new breathing.
                                This is how I imagine


your body: brown and surfacing, a changing shape
of grace and light to mirror
the foreboding chant of my own death,
or the true loss of a child in Korea
who goes West to become a child in America,
full of spectral images distracting him from
all the Korean trees, the clashing bodies,
all the animals and angels calling out his name.

# Portrait of the Korean Adoptee with Partial Alphabet

Air

A propeller swats through your chest when you think of her.
I landed in San Francisco, from Seoul, on October 12, 1971.
There was not a parade.

Birth Name

Could have been a cop, could have been an employee,
could have been my birth mother who named me: Lee Kwang Soo.

Cucumber kimchi

Please pass the cucumber kimchi. Please, the lemon soju.
Please, the blotted history.
Meat will keep you happy. You will think of me when you get hungry.

Demographics

He fails math when stories are introduced, begins to care less
about numbers and more about arcs, shadows, plots, and lies.

Daejeon

Outside the Express Train Station, in May, there are blooms
so light they could evaporate. You should go there to find out for yourself.

Dae-Won

He speaks *five* languages. We had beer and dried squid near KoRoot.
He is angel. Some kind of work is just holy.

Etymology

Eulogy. Egg. The world-wide wasted elegies.

Father

GOA'L

Good luck, good times, good boy, good banchan.

Holt

Imjing River. In Daejeon, we almost got lost.

Jennifer Kwon Dobbs, Jane Jeong Trenka.  Some kind of art is this pure.

KBS

Lee Kwang Soo is my birth name. I am 39. I will not go on.

May 6, 2008, I discovered I was born in or near Daejeon.

Nomenclature

Nam Dae Mun is not on fire in my dream.  There is no smoke.
9143 is my Holt case number.  You should see my photo.
I was plump and shocked.

Shim Soon-Duk.  Sun Yung Shin.

T
U
V

When one sense fails you, the other five will save your life.

X, ex, axes, axis. We are not evil.

You

You piece together what you can, when you can.
In the meantime, breathe as if your chest is an ocean.

# My California

Here, an olive votive keeps the sunset lit,
the Korean twenty-somethings talk about hyphens,

graduate school and good pot. A group of four at a window
table in Carpinteria discuss the quality of wines in Napa Valley versus Lodi.

Here, in my California, the streets remember the Chicano
poet whose songs still bank off Fresno's beer-soaked gutters

and almond trees in partial blossom. Here, in my California
we fish out long noodles from the pho with such accuracy

you'd think we'd done this before. In Fresno, the bullets
tire of themselves and begin to pray five times a day.

In Fresno, we hope for less of the police state and more of a state of grace.
In my California, you can watch the sun go down

like in your California, on the ledge of the pregnant
twenty-second century, the one with a bounty of peaches and grapes,

red onions and the good salsa, wine and chapchae.
Here, in my California, paperbacks are free,

farmer's markets are twenty-four hours a day and
always packed, the trees and water have no nails in them,

the priests eat well, the homeless eat well.
Here, in my California, everywhere is Chinatown,

everywhere is K-Town, everywhere is Armeniatown,
everywhere a Little Italy. Less confederacy.

No internment in the Valley.
Better history texts for the juniors.

In my California, free sounds and free touch. Free questions, free answers.
Free songs from parents and poets, those hopeful bodies of light.

# The Impossible Replication of Desire

How much delight before we collapse
How much earth in the lungs
How much wine

When we want more
When the weeds sprawl
It is not what you think

Think how fast some landscapes change
the lover, the gardener's grand idea,
the failing maple

the boat about to capsize
the correction
the hand's reflection

the impossible replication of weight
versus time
how it will never mean what you want

## Focus Theory

The black hair
the sweat on your neck,
the everlasting question.
Her lips on the wine glass.
Imagine all the beaches.
The curve of her hip.
More piano, more wind through the hair.

Once, I sang as if I were a small choir,
its voice indiscernible from the fire next door,
the birth of a boy right on time.

He is blessed now
with good luck and rice, balancing
on various borders for the rest of his life:
north and south
east and west
mother and mother.

Music will mitigate whatever you want.
The acoustic chord is a simple sound.
When I go to the next world,

I want one clear moment of focus.
I want lavender and waves.  There had better be waves.
I want to hear you, repeating over and over,
*if one sense fails you,*
*the other five will save your life.*

## Van Gogh Writes to Gaugin

When Van Gogh
wrote the letter to his friend, Gaugin,
and told him that he had felt well as of late,
that he had been painting olive trees with which he was pleased,
I want to know if he thought about death in that letter
and if death by his own hand was stirred away by those paints
in his hand, as now, I am trying not to think about death,
not by my own hand, but by my own disregard
for this abundant stillness, the calm sound in the center
of my stomach. They were oils, Van Gogh's olive trees.
And if the canvas could speak, it might choose not to.
It knew about genius and the madness involved with the trees,
the olives dancing on the branches like grenades.

# Kwi Ch'on

*for Ch'on Sang Pyong, 1930-1993*

Because after imprisonment, you could laugh
with your mouth so wide open, as if to swallow
the swirling bats of the CIA, because when you
disappeared in 1971, your friends thought
about your poems and you going back to heaven,
because I am dreaming of the sunset over Eurwangni
tonight, there is jujube tea in Insadong waiting for us.
Did you drink every hour of 1972?
And when they found you, unable
to remember your name but that you were a poet,
did you remember the answer to your own question?
That there is no answer at all but the request that
someone would find you in that fractured slur,
the tired lean and the pen your only possession,
that someone like her, with a language like food,
would know how tea can restore such fatigue?

# Fire

This is wind, air, or the absence of sufficient prayer,
the self-immolation of Thich Quang Duc
in Ho Chi Minh City, his friend dousing him in gasoline,
then the match, the wind, the air, the smoke, the fire.
This is the soul's whistling over the Vietnamese rooftops,
over the fathers and daughters, over the singed and the poor.
This is about campfires, suburban fires made by husbands
nearly dead or the soldier poet with the fire inside of him,
the pyromaniac down the block, and the Bolivian student
on the cusp of his own little revolution.
Some fires take a long time to blossom.
Chances are high you will not even notice the smoke.
You have passed many tall trees you should have stopped
to praise, many flowers whose names you should have learned,
many wood carvings steeped in Christ-like similarity.
Once, I broke down on the couch in my living room.
I thought I was going to die. This is different than the time
I broke down in front of my father at nineteen because
I did not want to die. My father saved me that night.

          What if the dead knew about each of our dreams?
What if they came back and said something about regret?
What if we knew the secrets of all the city's acoustics?
Would it matter if I told you I know nothing, that
there is no thing I want to tell you more
than how much I have fallen in love with this world
and all of its fires, its failures, its faith,
how I love all of your past fires, now ash?

# If We Are What We Eat

I am the raw jellied crab
in a small room in Insadong

I am pork browning on the barbecue
the lavender bud under the tongue

I am you and not you, the document
of black ink and number sequences

I am stacks of ham
and the dead scorpion in Beijing

the squid in Incheon, all the blossoms
from the tree in full bloom,

the trees and the bark, the wood
fire, the cold beer,

the fish I want to be but cannot be,
how I am not myself

but I am my skin, my hair,
slivers of black moon like ice.

# Freedom

Logic suspends it for only so long, given fire,
given water.  If we were more

elemental and less of the mind,
you could imagine the problems—skin,

revealed for what it is, less than what
we aspire to, given angels, given sky.

Look.  Start over.  We have
the open architecture for such capacity,

a new line, a real shift.
Do not let the roof or the net keep you from it.

Do not let that voice that sounds like your voice
keep you from it.  It is beyond that,

outside of your body,
aloft and everywhere you are.

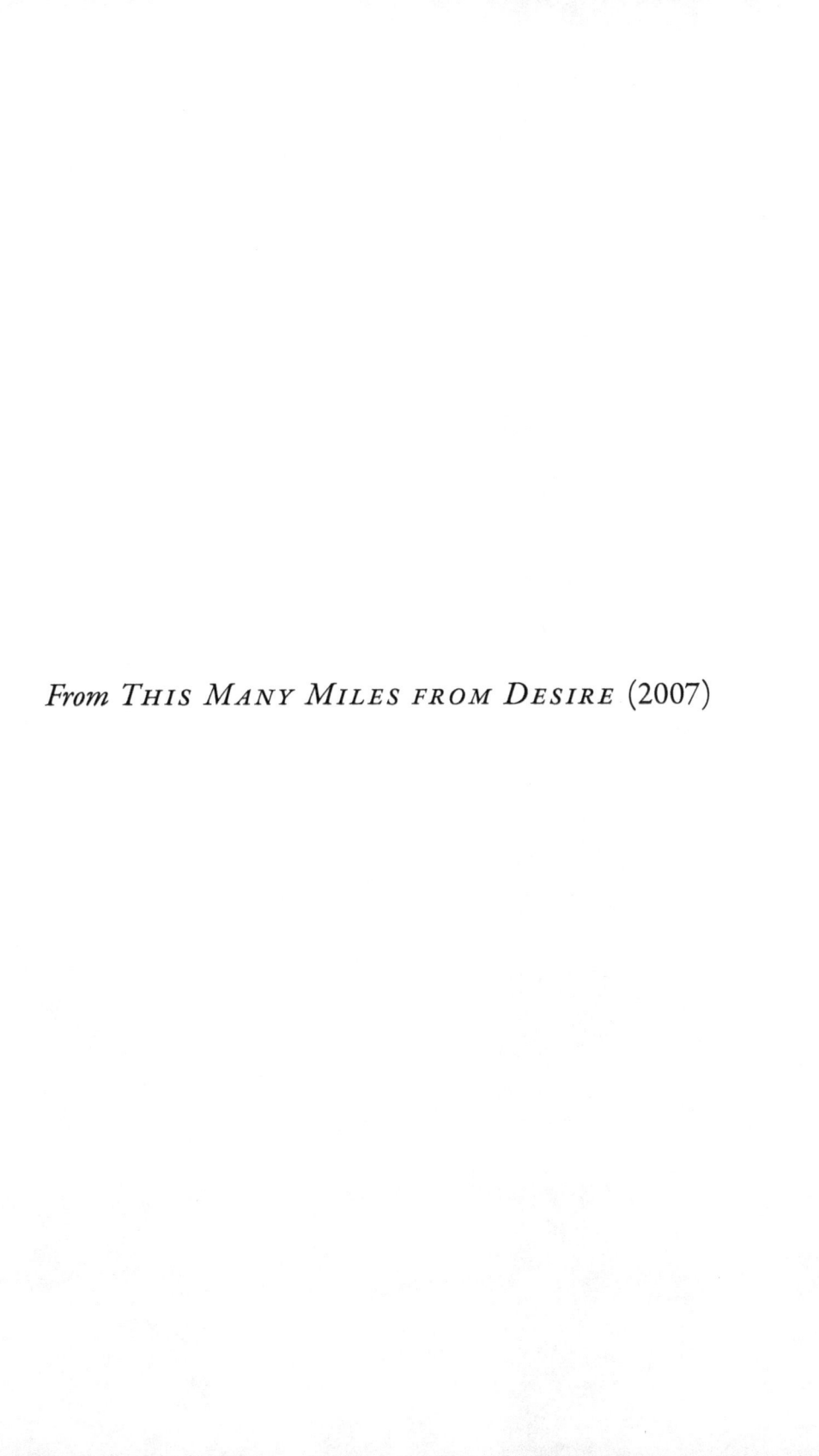

*From* THIS MANY MILES FROM DESIRE (2007)

## Ars Poetica

Yes, the ocean is Buddhist. And the foam
scrambling onto the beach is a symphony
of cymbals, small and caring like mothers
whispering to their children in the front pew,
*sssshhh*. Perhaps then the trees should
believe in God. Of course. How they reach
straight up after all those years like the Chinese
grandmothers rising at dawn, when the air's
cleanest, an orchestra of their own, stretching
toward the sun. None of this true. The ocean
is only Buddhist because a poet writes of it
that way—just like the grandmothers who keep
surfacing in his poems, usually dancing
somewhere near a body of water, blissfully.

## Adoption Music

I am learning to play the taiko, to feel
how leaves reappear in the trees with such ease.
One monk says this will teach me to hear
the variations of my name:
how my lover sighs it,
how a teacher grinded it out like a curse,
how your mother says it, drowning in a lake
before she leaves you. How it means somewhere
between mothers, not quite the rose
but not quite the roots. Like the woman
who finds you says, *Lee*, like a discovery—
one more child found in the world's history
of found children. How she said it like the echo
of one plucked E string, a clear pang of delight.

# Three Dreams of Korea: Notes on Adoption

1.

This one happens in morning
as a nearby crow wakes me,
calling *God, God, look at this*:
I am on the steps of a church,
wrapped in Monday's *Korea Times*
telling of the drought in Pusan.
You can live by the water
and still die of thirst, and I,
there on the cold brick steps,
am dying. But dying
means the presence of breath.
This one happens on Hangul Day,
Independence Day in Seoul,
where girls in purple satin
hanboks parade through
downtown streets. In this dream
I make eye contact with
every single one of them.
Another boy, a few years
older than I, rides
a tricycle in the parade,
trailing the girls.
He sees me. He winks,
as if he knows how
everything will end.

2.

This one happens in the evening
just as daylight surrenders to the moon,
and the flute of dusk arrives.

It is cool.
I am wrapped in a sky-blue blanket,
so whoever finds me thinks kindly
of whoever left me.
The one who finds me is a nun.
She opens the door, looking

beyond me
into the tired night,
then looks down.

She gasps softly.
She says, *ahneyong*, you sweet
beautiful child. She bends
down like an angel
and takes me
into her arms.

3.

This one happens in the cruelest moment
of the day, as heat curls flowers
into dirt. A man, drunk
with despair, screams at the sun.
His sorrow is a collage of
moths and ants, crawling
from his face to his chest.
I watch from the steps.
It is the year of the dog
and I am a part of it:
unable to speak
but an expert at listening:
to the old man from Laos who sits
on the steps two buildings down:
he is telling another man

how Hmong children become human
on the third day of life,
after the soul calling ceremony
and the burning of animal flesh.
He smokes from a pipe
and closes his eyes as he inhales.
I can hear all of this.
I can hear a woman rustling inside the church.
She is a dancer, so she speaks with her hands.
I hear her rise, sweetly
from her knees to her feet.
This means she believes
in dreams. I hear her
slide her hand, sweetly
along her hair. This means
she believes in the sun.
I hear her move towards me
and place her open palm on the door.
This means she welcomes me.
This means she believes
in the miracle of possibility.

## Vision as Delicacy

A tender balance—the glassy lens of your eye
against what we endure: the allergic explosion

swelling the lids, the unfiltered sun on the river—

Often, the eye becomes a delicacy—the man of honor
eating the fish eye in east China, how the eye watches him,

hopes for him, even in its fleshy socket.

In the marketplace, that eye on the side of the dead pig's head,
white and round and ready for the fire,

reminds a man of the delicate nature of love,
the circular nature of vision at its best,

a fusion of death and light. Close both
eyes softly. Notice the weight of the lids,

the heightened sense of your own miraculous breath

making its way out. How startling to
open your eyes and take the world in,

one amazing vision at a time.

# Salvation

The blues is what mothers do not tell their sons,
in church or otherwise, how their bodies forgave
them when their spirits gave in, how you salvage love
by praying for something acoustic, something clean

and simple like the ideal room, one with a shelf
with your three favorite books and a photo
from your childhood, the one of you with the
big grin before you knew about the blues.

I wonder what songs my birth mother sang in
the five months she fed me before she left me
on the steps of a church in South Korea.
I wonder if they sounded like Sarah Chang's

quivering bow, that deep chant of a mother
saying goodbye to her son. Who can really say?
Sometimes all we have is the blues. The blues means
finding a song in the abandonment, one

you can sing in the middle of the night when
you remember that your Korean name, Kwang Soo
Lee, means bright light, something that can illuminate
or shine, like tears, little drops of liquefied God,

glistening down your brown face. I wonder
what songs my birth mother sings and if she sings
them for me, what stories her body might tell.
I have come to believe that the blues is the body's

salvation, a chorus of scars to remind you
that you are here, not where you feared you would be,
but here, flawed, angelic, and full of light.
I believe that the blues is the spirit's wreckage,

examined and damaged but whole again, more full
and prepared than it's ever been, quiet and still,
just as it was always meant to be.

# Raison d'Être

This is the beginning. Almost anything can happen.
On stage, the house lights dim and a curtain rises.
The first tomato of the year.  A boom of thunder.
This is where you realize you are falling in love.
This is January, the green digital clock beeping
you into Monday at 6:00 a.m., 6:00 a.m., 6:00 a.m.
This is the first time you saw her and the last time
you saw her. This is first guitar chord of the opening
song on the first date of a month-long tour.
The cool sand on a clean beach. This is where
you learn how to ask questions
in order to get what you want.

This is the middle. The stomach moaning for lunch,
a child with bloody elbows, a thrown stone beginning
its descent. This is the turning point of the film
where you think, *this is starting to get good.*
This is the gas station bathroom on a five-hour drive.
This is the bridge, the refrain, the leap from a perfectly
good plane. This is the batch of tomatoes that becomes
a gift for a friend. Here is a time to think, *my God
what have I done?* Make your substitutions.
Get the right players on the field.
This is the apology, suspended
in midair like a cloud.

And this, this is the end. This is the guitarist
smashing the amp, the last lip of the sun over the hills.
Here we discover our reason for being, the black mascara
on a widow's cheek, and the solemn bow to the crowd.

Here is the moon, December, midnight. This is Friday,
the exhale after too long a wait. This is the coda,
the swan howling at the lake, a moon bloated
with deathbed prayers. This is like a beginning.
A circle of sorts. Here is where you realize love
assumes the shapes of flowers in damp backyards,
denying the temptation to wilt.

## How to Spend a Birthday

Light a match.  Watch the blue part

                                              flare like a shocked pinata

                         from the beating
                         into the sky,

                             watch how fast thin

wood burns & turns toward the skin,

the olive-orange skin of your thumb

                                   & let *it* burn, too.

Light a fire.  Drown out the singing cats.

Let the drunken mariachis blaze their way,

streaking like crazed hyenas

over a brown hill, just underneath

a perfect birthday moon.

# The Violinst

*after Stephen Wunrow's photograph of Sarah Chang,*
*Asian-American violinist*

Sarah, I've every desire to feel your hands
and come to the ancient conversation between you
and Max Bruch there, steady on the bow.
Here is the definition of softness, the way you hold
the neck just as you did when you were eight
for the New York Philharmonic.
If you let go, would the music float to heaven?
Or would it flutter around my ear, brushing
itself against me like a child?
Sarah, if I had an hour with you
I would pray for the notes
we have the fortune to absorb
and let them stand
for the one hundred ways
I imagine your smile, curling at the end
of the concerto, blowing the roof into the sky.

# Belief

I go around believing everything. I believe that
the leaves turn orange in October out of fatigue.
I believe that an acoustic can heal.
I believe just a little in all of your Gods
and even more in the compassion with which you
praise them. I believe what Nietzsche said, that
without music, life would be a mistake.
I believe in my own mistakes and deities.
The way they gather around me at night
like feeding birds. I believe in the sound of my breath.
I have discovered the pleasure of belief, the surrender
of the intellectual, and the moment when thought
gives way to the heart. I believe what Paz said, that
the many who read poems worm their way into
immeasurable realities, and in the mirror of words,
discover their own infinity. I believe in manifestos.
I believe in collecting and keeping and giving back.
I believe in the day I gathered fifteen petals of a fallen
pink rose, and let them stand for my failures and
aspirations.  I believe in the strength of a tired
mother, reading poems in secrecy,
discovering the sound of her voice.

# A Thousand Saxophones

*After Hurricane Katrina—A Poem for the Living and the Dead*

You can live by the water and still die of thirst.
I said you can live by the water and still die of thirst
or the worst nightmare come true:
that body of water taking over the bodies.
Sometime, tonight, see which echoes most—
a whisper or a scream. Make it something beautiful,
like, *we will endure* or *yes, I love you.* Sometime,
tonight, think of water—how it purifies or terrifies,
cleanses, gives and takes away—think how fast
some things can rise—water, fear, the intensity of a prayer.
Officials in New Orleans said they want to save the living.
I hope they do. But I hope they can also honor the dead.
On Bourbon Street, there were over 3,000 musicians employed
on any given day. Last night, before I fell asleep,
I imagined what a thousand saxophones
would sound like if they all played together—
one thousand saxophones, different songs,
different tempos, Dixieland, Miles Davis.
Maybe it would sound like birds or bombs,
planes or preachers praising the Word
on a hot Sunday and the congregation saying Amen,
some people whispering it, some people screaming it.
Maybe it would sound like lightning tearing
open the sky or a thousand books slammed shut after
a horrible conclusion, or a thousand children crying
for their mothers or fathers. Last night, I thought, how far
would a thousand saxophones echo from New Orleans or Biloxi?
Would we hear them in Fresno? Could we imagine the sound?

Could Baton Rouge? Could Washington D.C.?
I don't know what I should tell you.
But I feel like the saints are marching.
They are singing a slow, deep, and beautiful song,
waiting for us to join in.

## Yoga On the Beach

When surfers depart & the sun gives way
To the moon, it is holy. Occasional seagulls.
A sleek seal watches. Tenderly
With eyes closed, a woman with no clothes
Suspends the air with her finest act of balance
To date. When everything falls away
See how she gathers the birds. See how
She gathers their sweetness. On the tongue.
With the skin. See how she carves in the sand,
*This is where everything begins.*

# In the Tower District, Fresno

There are fragments
of everything. An artist draws

the sun on the verge of arrival.
Andres the poet says you can't fight

this heat, it's too large for us,
so pleasure must be discovered

in the submission. Two boys walk,
one in front of the other, holding him

by a leash. A Chihuahua smiles
at the basil from Piemonte's, approves

and nods at the smokers
in front of the Revue. A Mexican

boy rides a low-rider bicycle slowly.
As his feet complete a rotation—

Coolio finishes a verse.
No one sweats here,

where small dogs rule
and a young woman

with swirling tattoos excavates
her lover's mouth,

her tongue stud sparkling
from the sinking sun.

# Ghost in a Museum

The ghost of Carlos Baca Flor sighs
near the tall arches, the climbing windows stained
centuries ago, literally ages—Bronze, Middle,

Stone. And the woman at the café counter
sighs, reads Monday's news of Peru. A young boy
sweeps. Hardly any dust here. And there,
over by the window,
a woman thinks.

What dreams did Manuel Ortega have
the night he finished a painting? In my daydream,
the ghost of Carlos Baca Flor stands
near the tall arches.

Do you go to a museum to fall in love, to fall
in new love again, to forget, or to float?
Yes, it is like floating, being in a museum—
the texture of Uncle Ho's shirt,
the Lilies.

What would Vincent Van Gogh say to Ho Chi Minh
over coffee in Hue?
Would Van Gogh know more about tanks
than Uncle Ho would of flowers?

And whose self-portraits are most accurate,
the blind or the mad?

What kind of stories will your home tell,
the verandas keep,
those birds rehash into the wind?

## What Is Sacred

I have no idea what priests
dream of on Christmas Eve, what prayer

a crippled dog might whine before the shotgun.
I have no more sense of what is sacred

than a monk might have, sweeping the temple
floor, slow gestures of honor to the left,

the right. Maybe the leaf of grass tells us
what is worthwhile. Maybe it tells us nothing.

Perhaps a sacred moment is a photograph
you look at over and over again, the one

of you and her, hands lightly clasped like you
did before prayer became necessary, the one

with the sinking cathedral in Mexico City rising up
behind you and a limping man frozen in time

to the right of you, the moment when she touched
your bare arm for the first time, her fingers

like cool flashes of heaven.

# ACKNOWLEDGMENTS

The author would like to express his deepest gratitude to the editors and publishers of the following journals and presses, where some of the poems in this book first appeared:

Academy of American Poets and *MiGoZine*: "The Birds Outside My Window Sing During a Pandemic"
*Atticus Review*: "Mother Clouds"
*BOOM California*: "Abecedarian Love Song for Street Food"
*Hanging Loose*: "In Praise of Late Wonder"
*Huizache*: "Stars" and "Acclimation"
*San Diego Poetry Annual*: "Partial Crown in Praise of Absent Sounds"

First collected in *Scar and Flower* (Word Poetry Press)

*Columbia Poetry Review*: "Fatigue"
*Gramma Poetry Daily*: "What I Hear When I Hear You in My Head," "What I Hear After the Massacre and What I Mistake for My Heart," and "Flight"
*Hyphen*: "Echolocation," "Repertoire," and "Sun"
*Lantern Review*: "The House is Quiet, Except"
*Leaf by Leaf*: "Stars" and "Lecture"
*Penumbra*: "Manifesto" and "Dear_____,"
*Spectrum*: "Strawberries"
*Taos International Journal of Poetry and Art*: "Truths"
*The Normal School*: "Rose"

First collected in *Gardening Secrets of the Dead* (WordTech Editions)

*Cha*: "Spectral Questions of the Body" and "If We Are What We Eat"
*Highway 99: A Literary Journey through California's Great Central Valley*: "In the Tower District, Fresno"
*Mascara Literary Review*: "Self-Portrait"
*More than Soil, More than Sky: The Modesto Poets*: "Freedom"
*One for the Money: The Sentence as Poetic Form*: Editors Christopher Buckley and Gary Young

*Poetry Foundation* online: "How to Spend a Birthday"
*The Journal of Korean Adoption Studies*: "Kwi Ch'on," "Light,"
*The Packinghouse Review*: "Gardening Secrets of the Dead"
*ZYZZYVA*: "My California"
"Stars" was displayed as part of the art exhibit "Born into Identity: The Asian Pacific American Adoptees Experience," at The Wing Luke Museum of the Asian Pacific American Experience in Seattle.

First collected in *This Many Miles from Desire* (WordTech Editions)

*Berkeley Poetry Review*: "Georgia"
*Haight Ashbury Literary Journal*: "Backs," "Crossword," "Dreamer," "What Is Sacred"
*Hawai'i Pacific Review*: "Lines"
*Hurricane Blues: Poems About Katrina and Rita*: "A Thousand Saxophones"
*Inside English*: "Gravity"
*Korean Quarterly*: "The Violinst"
*Many Mountains Moving*: "Three Dreams of Korea: Notes on Adoption"
*MiPOesias*: "Korean Adoptee Returns to Seoul," "Korean Adoptee Daydreams"
*Penumbra*: "Raison D'etre"
*Peralta Press*: "Ars Poetica"
*Quercus Review*: "Four Types of Jeong"
*Willow Review*: "Adoption Music"

Several poems first appeared in a chapbook of poems, *Coping with Vertigo*, published by Talent House Press: "Air," "Belief," "For Andres and Eleanor," "Slowness," "Yoga on the Beach."

# Author's Note

My most heartfelt, deepest gratitude:

Lisa, for your encouragement, support, first reader expertise, and love in all things, writing and life. To Suzhen, for your light, love, and feedback expertise. You are loved. To my parents, Georgia and Newby Herrick, for always being there, for your love and support, and for giving me a love of books, reading, and creativity, and for everything. To my sister Holly, Scott, and Ella, for your love and support. To the Lee family, for everything.

Optimism One, for your decades of friendship and support. Zoua, Curtis, John and Michelle.

Juan Felipe Herrera, Andrés Montoya, Marisol Baca, Brynn Saito, Joseph Rios, David Campos, Juan Luis Guzmán, Connie Hales, David Good, Michael Roberts, Kenneth Chacón, Daniel Chacón, Steven Church, Von Torres, Bryan Medina, Mia Barraza Martinez, Pos Moua, Mai Der Vang, Anthony Cody, Soul Vang, and Fresno poets and writers, past and present, for their support, encouragement, and inspiration.

Brian Turner, Patricia Smith, Suzanne Roberts, June Sylvester Saraceno, Faylita Hicks, Gailmarie Pahmeier, Laura Wetherington, Pablo Cartaya, Carolyn Forché, Gayle Brandeis, and the University of Nevada, Reno at Lake Tahoe low-residency MFA program for their support, encouragement, and inspiration.

Amy Uyematsu, Ishle Yi Park, Lorna Dee Cervantes, Chris Buckley, Timothy Liu, and Ed Bok Lee for their support and encouragement.

The Korean adoption community and adopted poets and writers for their friendship, support, and inspiration, including Sun Yung Shin, Jennifer Kwon Dobbs, Susan Ito, Kim Sunée, Matt Salesses, Jane Jeong Trenka, and Leah Silvieus. To Korea. To my first mother and first father.

All of my teachers, for their wisdom, patience, encouragement, and guidance. To the editors and publishers of my previous work, for their belief in my writing. To my colleagues and students and everyone at Fresno City College, Sierra Nevada College, the University of Nevada, Reno at Lake Tahoe, and Kundiman.

Governor Newsom for his trust and belief by appointing me as the tenth California Poet Laureate, and his staff, First Partner Jennifer Siebel Newsom and her staff, for everything.

The Fresno Arts Council, including Andrea Mele and Lilia Gonzáles-Chávez, and the California Arts Council, including former Executive Director Jonathan Moscone, Charlie O'Malley, Kristin Margolis, and the entire team.

Chryss Yost and David Starkey and Gunpowder Press for their enthusiasm and belief in my work and for bringing this book to life.

Every reader of my poems, adoptees everywhere, friends and supporters, and each poet, writer, whom I have met over the years, thank you.

Lee Herrick is the tenth California Poet Laureate and the first Asian American to serve in the role. He is the author of *In Praise of Late Wonder: New and Selected Poems* and three other books of poems: *Scar and Flower, Gardening Secrets of the Dead,* and *This Many Miles from Desire.* He co-edited *The World I Leave You: Asian American Poets on Faith and Spirit* and *Afterlives: An AGNI Portfolio of Asian Adoptee Diaspora Writing.* His poems appear widely in anthologies such as *Here: Poems for the Planet,* with an introduction by the Dalai Lama, and *Indivisible: Poems of Social Justice,* with a foreword by Common, among others. He previously served as Fresno Poet Laureate. Born in Daejeon, Korea, and adopted as an infant, he lives and teaches in Fresno, California.

www.ingramcontent.com/pod-product-compliance
Lightning Source LLC
Chambersburg PA
CBHW031421120626
46545CB00006B/2218